Simon's Cat

Simon's Cat in Kitten Chaos

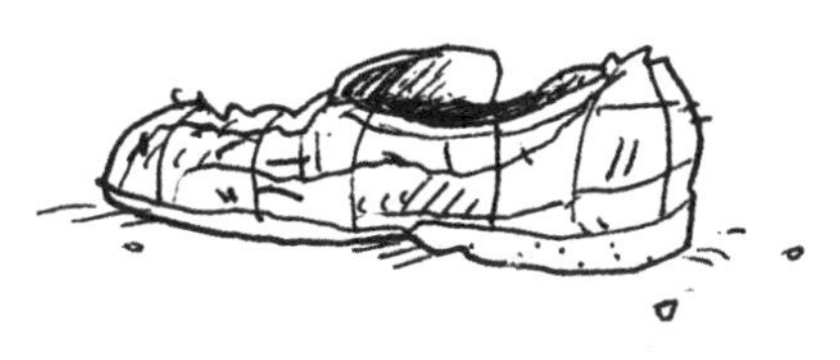

by Simon Tofield

Published in the United States by Akashic Books
Published by arrangement with Canongate Books Ltd, 14 High Street, Edinburgh EH1 1TE

ISBN-13: 978-1-61775-158-5
Library of Congress Control Number: 2012952044
Typeset by Simon's Cat

First Akashic Books printing

Akashic Books
PO Box 1456
New York, NY 10009
info@akashicbooks.com
www.akashicbooks.com

Printed in China

This book is dedicated
to Don Evans

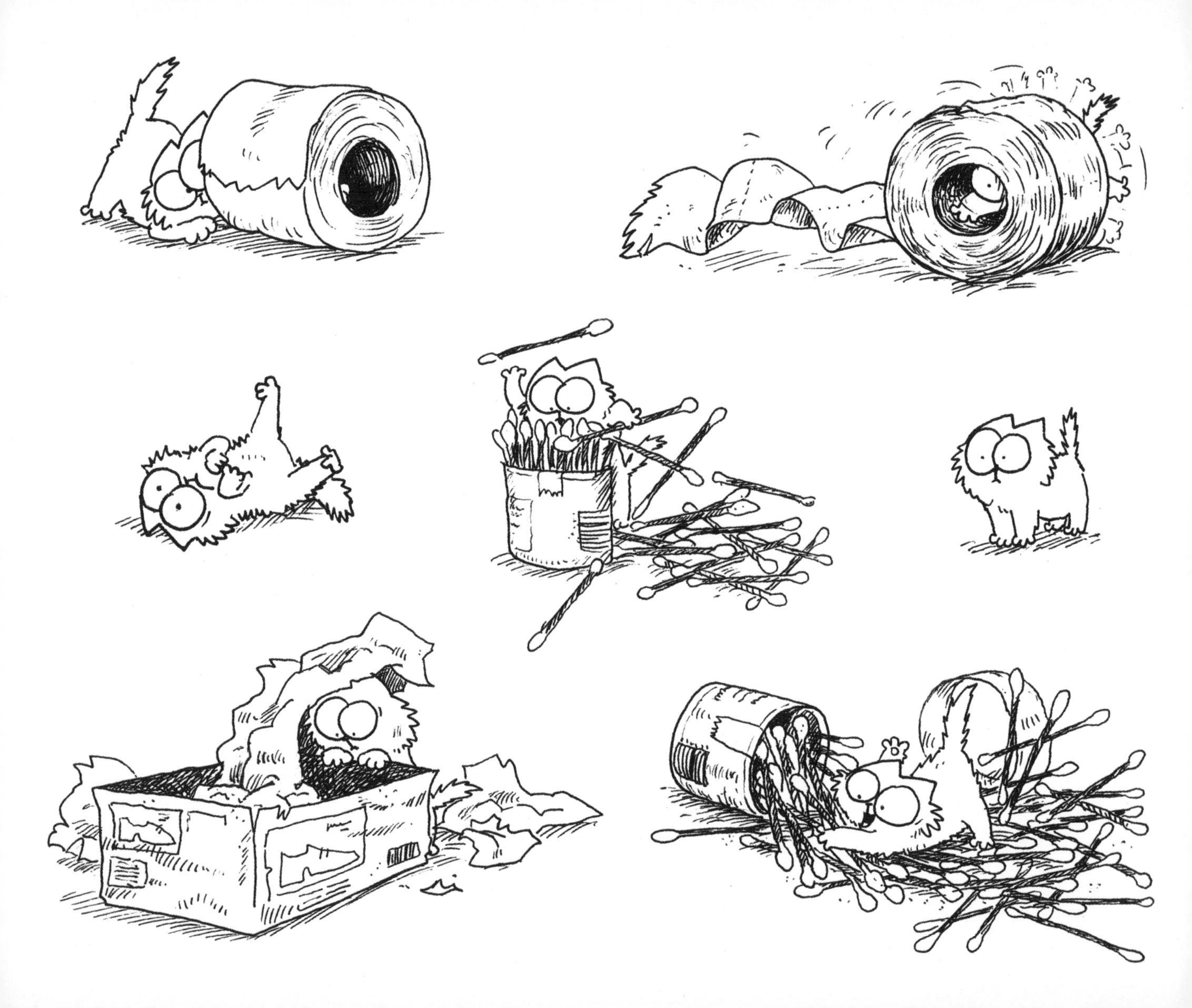

P

S
P

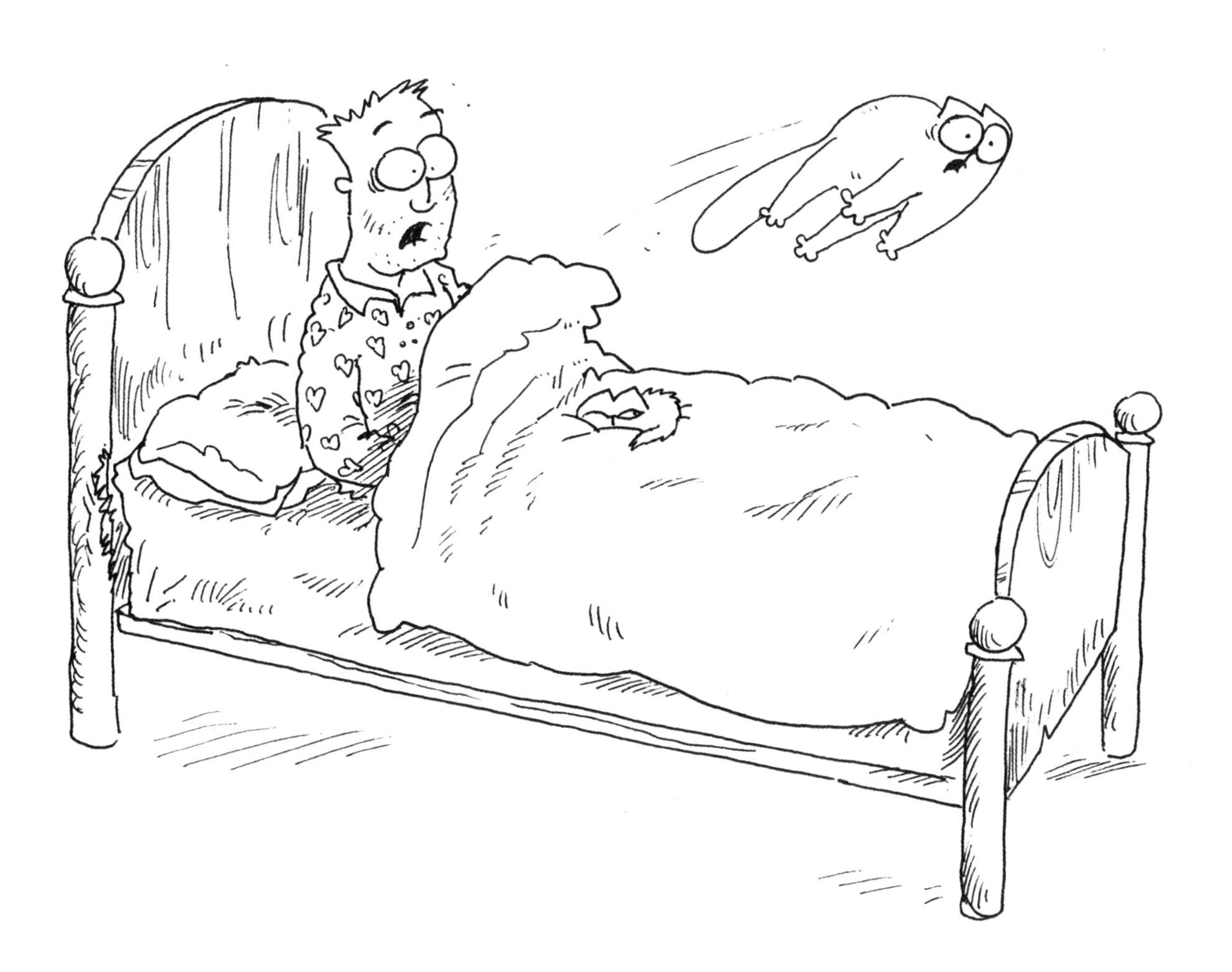

Z Z Z

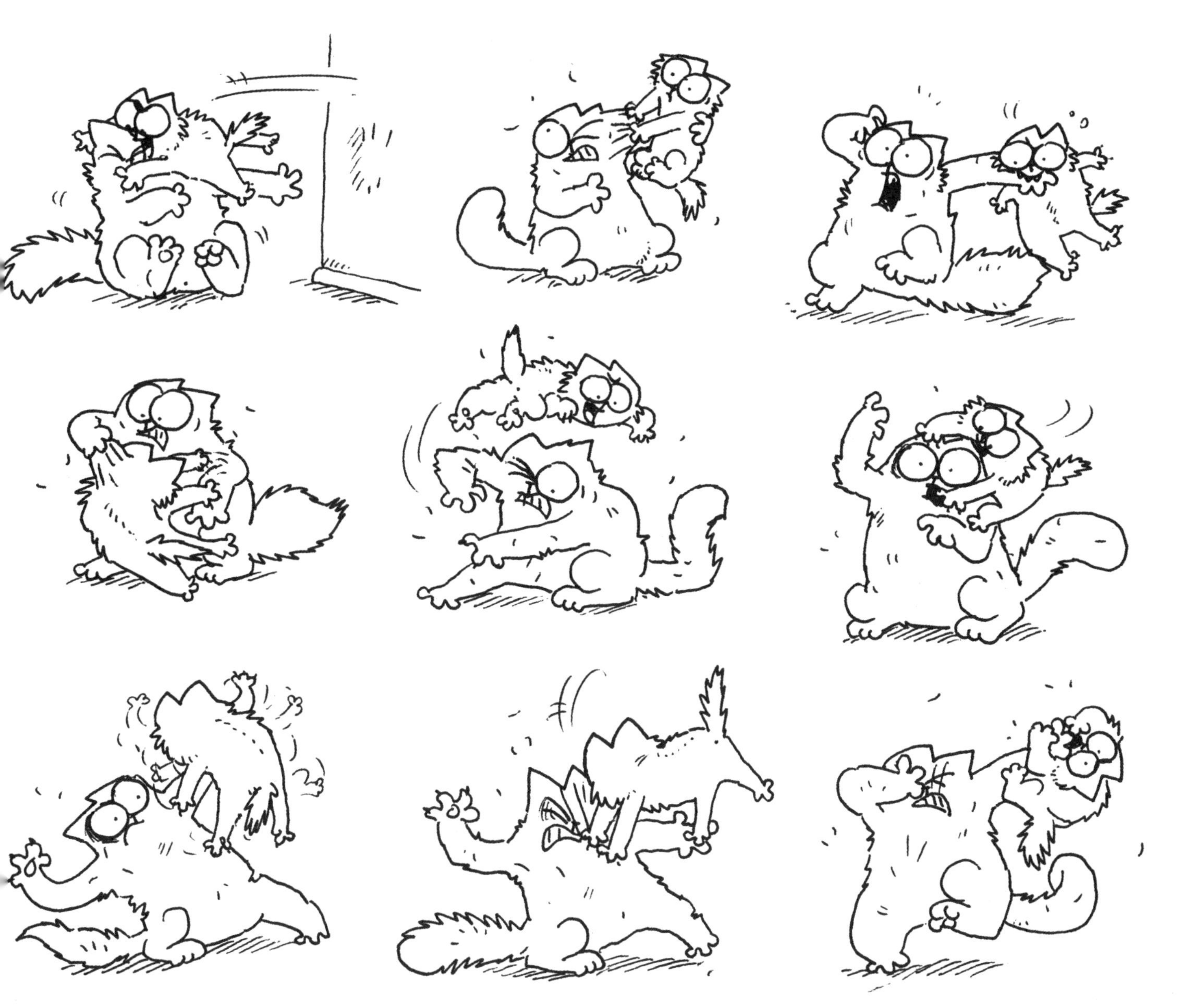

z z z
z z z
z z z

Simon Draws : Simon's Cat

1:

I'm going to show you how to draw Simon's Cat. Let's start by drawing two big round eyes.

2:

Simon's Cat is always hungry, so I draw him with a big wide-open mouth, then shade it in.

3:

Next, the cat's ears: you can draw both ears with a single line shaped like the capital letter "M."

4:

I'm drawing the classic "Feed Me" pose, so here's his paw pointing into his gaping mouth.

5:

I draw the other three legs next.
He's got little dumpy legs and paws.

6:

Simon's Cat has a great big
fat fluffy tail.

7:

I like to add hatching lines to
show a ground shadow.

8:

Finally, let's give him his food bowl.
MEOW!

Simon Draws : The Kitten

1:

Now I'll show you how to draw the kitten. Start by drawing the eyes.

2:

The kitten (like the cat) has a small nose and mouth.

3:

The kitten has the same "M"-shaped ears as the cat.

4:

Unlike the cat, the kitten has big fluffy cheeks.

5:

Kittens have short legs, but surprisingly big feet.

6:

Kittens have huge heads but tiny bodies.

7:

The kitten has a little tail which points straight up when he's happy.

8:

Finally, let's add some shading for his ground shadow. MEW!

Simon Draws : The Hedgehog

1:

First draw the hedgehog's big round eyes, then a pointy snout.

2:

I draw the back next, but use a dashed line to show his spines.

3:

He has a rounded pear-shaped body and a fat belly.

4:

I draw him with tiny little arms.

He also has small rodent-like feet.

I draw another dashed line to split the body and chest areas.

Fill in the back area with dots; he's got lots of prickly spines.

8:

Finally, I give him a little ground shadow.

Simon Draws : The Dog

1:

To draw the dog, overlap the eyes slightly, then draw a long nose.

2:

The dog is always alert, so I draw his ears pricked up.

3:

He has a big floppy tongue lolling out of his mouth. I draw three teeth.

4:

I give the dog a collar, then draw his body. His chest sticks out slightly.

5:

The body leads down to long bony legs.

6:

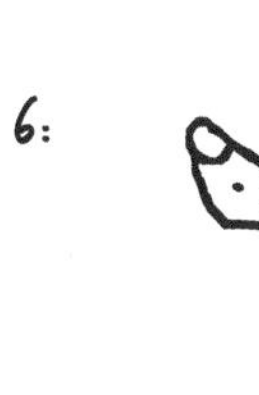

He's excited and wags his pointy tail.

Jack Russells are full of energy. I like to draw them shivering and shaking.

8:

Finally, let's give him a stick to play with.

Simon Draws : A Rabbit

1:

Start drawing the rabbit with round eyes, then a little "U"-shaped nose.

2:

Just under the nose, draw the rabbit's little mouth.

3:

Straight up above the eyes draw two big rabbit ears.

4:

Draw two tiny feet: these make the rabbit look very cute.

5:

Next I draw a very simple pear-shaped body.

6:

The fluffy tail is drawn just behind the body.

7:

Rabbits have these great big hind legs and feet.

8:

Finally, I give the bunny a ground.

Simon Draws : Simon

1:

To draw Simon (that's me), start with two eyes and the nose.

2:

It's a cartoon of myself: spiky hair, mouth, face, and collar.

3:

In this pose I'll be kneeling down, so I draw my arm stretching to the floor.

4:

I draw the hand flat on the ground with the fingers spread apart.

5:

In this crouched pose, I draw my legs bent double under my body.

6:

The other arm is raised, clenched fingers gripping onto something.

7:

In the raised hand I draw a cat toy, a stick with a fluffy end.

8:

Finally, I add movement lines around the toy and a ground shadow.

Simon Draws : A Mouse

1:

Start drawing the mouse with big round eyes.

2:

This mouse has a snout that curves upward toward the end.

3:

This is a wood mouse so I'll draw quite large round ears.

4:

Two small front paws will make him look very cute indeed.

5:

The mouse has a pear-shaped body, with hind legs and feet similar to the hedgehog.

6:

The mouse has a long curved tail.

I like to add some ribbed lines to the tail.

8:

Finally, I give the mouse his ground shadow.

Simon Draws : A Frog

1:

The frog starts with big round eyes.

2:

Below the eyes I then draw a big sad-looking mouth.

3:

The back of the frog's body is smooth, the front bulges out.

4:

The front legs are thin at the top, then fatter at the bottom. They curve inward under the body.

5:

The rear legs are much bigger.

6:

I add striped markings to the back legs.

7:

Now I'll draw some black dots on the frog's back.

8:

Finally, I give the frog a ground shadow too.

Acknowledgments

Everyone at Stray Cat Rescue for their ongoing work, Zoe Herbert-Jackson, Ross Walker, the Simon's Cat team, Mike Cook, Nigel Pay, Daniel Greaves, Mike Bell, Nick Davies and the Canongate team, Johnny Temple and the Akashic team, Robert Kirby and Duncan Hayes at UA, and, of course, my inspirational cats.

For all your Simon's Cat goodies, check out the webshop at

www.simonscat.com